Dear Friends,

The life of a classroom hamster like me is full of adventure, and it's also FUN-FUN-FUN. My classmates in Room 26 of Longfellow School learn a lot from our teacher, Mrs. Brisbane. We also share a lot of laughs, especially Stop-Giggling-Gail and I-Heard-That-Kirk. I've been writing down all the unsqueakably funny jokes and riddles I've heard in the little notebook I keep hidden in my cage. I also love to make puzzles and games in my notebook. Now I've put them all together so you can laugh and play along with me.
Have fun!

Your friend,
Humphrey

Read all of Humphrey's Adventures!

Nonfiction books featuring Humphrey

Humphrey's Tiny Tales for young readers

Betty G. Birney

Humphrey's

Book of FUN-FUN-FUN

PUFFIN BOOKS
An Imprint of Penguin Group (USA)

PUFFIN BOOKS
Published by the Penguin Group
Penguin Group (USA) LLC
375 Hudson Street
New York, New York 10014

USA * Canada * UK * Ireland * Australia
New Zealand * India * South Africa * China

penguin.com
A Penguin Random House Company

First published in the United Kingdom as *Humphrey's Book of Fun-Fun-Fun*
by Faber and Faber Limited, 2010, and *Humphrey's Book of Ha-Ha-Ha*
by Faber and Faber Limited, 2011
Published as one volume by Puffin Books,
an imprint of Penguin Young Readers Group, 2013

Puffin Books ISBN 978-0-14-750951-2

Printed in the United States of America

3 5 7 9 10 8 6 4

Humphrey's

Book of FUN-FUN-FUN

Humphrey's Silly School Jokes

As the classroom hamster in Room 26 of Longfellow School, I know school can be **FUN-FUN-FUN**. But these school jokes are even funnier!

Q. What kind of pliers do you use in arithmetic?
A. Multipliers.

TEACHER: What do you get if you add 5,829 and 8,652, then subtract 548 and divide the answer by 23?
STUDENT: A headache!

Q. What kind of meals do math teachers eat?
A. Square meals.

Q. What is the fruitiest class?
A. History, because it's full of dates.

Q. Why did the music teacher need a ladder?

A. To reach the high notes.

Q. Why did the teacher wear sunglasses?

A. Because his class was so bright.

I think my class is the brightest bunch of all—and I'm sure Mrs. Brisbane would agree!

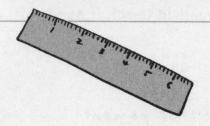

Q. What did the pencil say to the eraser?
A. "Take me to your ruler."

Q. What do elves do after school?
A. Gnomework.

Q. What do elves learn in school?
A. The elf-abet.

Teacher: Can anyone tell me what wind is?
STUDENT: Air in a hurry?

Q. What did the tree say to the math teacher?

A. "Gee, I'm a tree!"

It took a little while for me to work this out. I wrote it out in my notebook and then got it—GEOMETRY!

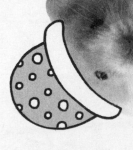

Teacher: Want to hear the story about the broken pencil?

STUDENT: No, thanks, I'm sure it has no point.

Q. What happened when the class started writing poetry?

A. Things went from bad to verse.

That reminds me of the time my classmates wrote poems to recite at the Poetry Festival—in fact, everyone's rhymes were GREAT-GREAT-GREAT!

Here's one of mine:
Roses are red,
Violets are blue,
I guess that now,
I'm a poet, too!

Q. What is a snake's favorite subject?
A. Hisstory.

Q. What else do snakes learn at school?
A. How to read and writhe.

TEACHER: Can anyone tell me what a volcano is?
STUDENT: A mountain with hiccups.

TEACHER: What happened at the Boston Tea Party?
STUDENT: I don't know, I wasn't invited!

TEACHER: Why does the Statue of Liberty stand in New York Harbor?
STUDENT: Because it can't sit down.

TEACHER: What do you call the outside of a tree?

STUDENT: I don't know.

TEACHER: Bark.

STUDENT: Woof! Woof!

Woof!

Q. Where did the math teacher eat his lunch?

A. At the times table.

That reminds me—which tables do you never have to learn? DINNER TABLES, of course!

Q. Why would Snow White make a great teacher?
A. She's the fairest in the land.

Q. Which snake does best in math class?
A. An adder.

Mrs. Brisbane knows so much about the world—but I don't think she's ever heard history and geography told QUITE like this!

Q. How was the Roman Empire cut in half?

A. With a pair of Caesars.

Q. What game did ancient Egyptian children like playing?

A. Mummies and Deadies.

Q. What was the favorite music of Egyptian mummies?
A. Wrap!

Q. Did the ancient Greeks hunt bear?
A. Not in the winter!

Q. What do you get if you cross a mouse with a Roman Emperor?
A. Julius Cheeser.

Being a hamster, my favorite foods are veggies—but I just love a "CHEESY" joke!

Q. Why were King Arthur's men so tired?
A. He had a lot of sleepless knights.

Q. Who made King Arthur's round table?
A. Sir-Cumference.

Q. Who stole from the rich to pay for the bows in his hair?
A. Ribbon Hood.

That reminds me of CINDERELLA, who was just no good at soccer. She kept running away from the ball!

Q. Who invented fractions?
A. Henry the 1/8th.

Q. When did Queen Victoria die?
A. Just a few days before they buried her.

Q. Who succeeded the first president of the U.S.A.?
A. The second one.

Q. Where was the Declaration of Independence signed?
A. At the bottom.

Q. Where do all pencils come from?
A. Pennsylvania.

Q. What city cheats at exams?
A. Peking!

Q. What's purple and 5,000 miles long?
A. The Grape Wall of China.

I've never been to CHINA. I'd sure love to roll my ball along the Great Wall one day!

Q. What leans to one side and has a cheese and tomato topping?
A. The Leaning Tower of Pizza.

Q. Why did the student take a ladder to school?
A. Because it was high school!

Q. Why was the math book sad?
A. Because he had so many problems.

Q. What subject do moths like best?
A. Moth-ematics.

What's in a Name?

My friends in Room 26 of Longfellow School all have very different personalities. Some are quiet, some are noisy, and one of them is **VERY-VERY-VERY** giggly! Our teacher, Mrs. Brisbane, has special names for her students. Can you remember them? Find the missing words in the column on the right, and write them in the correct space to complete my friends' names.

1. _____-Up-Sayeh

2. Raise-Your-_____Heidi

3. Pay-_____Art

4. Lower-Your-_____A.J.

5. Stop-_____Gail

6. _____-It-Please-Richie

7. Sit-_____Seth

8. Wait-for-the-_____Garth

STILL

ATTENTION

GIGGLING

REPEAT

SPEAK

HAND

BELL

VOICE

See answers on page 216

Mrs. Brisbane's Spelling Test

I do love to take Mrs. Brisbane's weekly spelling tests! I write all my answers in my little notebooks, and, even though I'm not as good a speller as Speak-Up-Sayeh, I usually get most of them right! Test your spelling skills in one of Mrs. Brisbane's tests. Just (circle) the correct word in each pair. **WARNING**: they get harder as they go along!

1. write/rite
2. lite/light
3. little/litle
4. scool/school
5. woud/would
6. beak/beek
7. different/diffrent
8. becaws/because
9. beleive/believe
10. Wednesday/Wendsday

See answers on page 217

Aldo's Antics Dot-to-Dot

My good friend Aldo the custodian loves to talk to me while he cleans Room 26, and he also does amazing tricks. Do you know what he is balancing on his fingertip? Join the dots to find out!

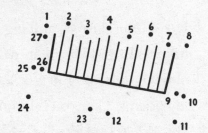

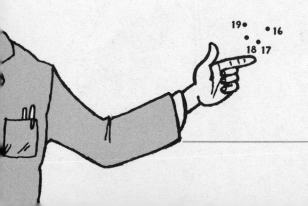

Humphrey's Rhyme Time

Help! Our class is studying poetry with Mrs. Brisbane this week, and I've been writing my own little verses in my notebook. But I've left out one word in each of my poems. Can you fill in the missing rhyming word, **PLEASE-PLEASE-PLEASE**?

1. You know, I think it's really cool,
To be a student at Longfellow _____.

2. Aldo the caretaker cleans up our room.
He uses a mop,
a bucket and _____.

3. One time, I had a
lovely float
On Potter's Pond,
aboard a _____.

SS GOLDEN HAMSTER

4. My big train adventure was FUN-FUN-FUN,
But I was happy when it was _____ .

5. Og is my fellow
classroom pet.
He lives in a tank and likes
to get _____ .

6. I have many good friends, including Og,
But I'm not a big fan of Miranda's pet _____ .

(Hey, can you remember the name of Miranda's
big hairy pet?)

See answers on page 218

Humphrey's Secret Code

Shhh!

A

B

C

D

E

F

G

H

I

J

K

L

M

N

O

P

Q

R

S

T

U

V

W

X

Y

Z

I'm very good at keeping secrets—and I love secret codes. They're **FUN-FUN-FUN** to solve! In my notebook I've been making up my own secret code using pictures of things that I like. And now I've written *you* a message. It's a saying I heard from a great book Mrs. Brisbane read to us by a famous writer called Robert Louis Stevenson. I think it's very true. Can you figure out what it is? Write each letter in the space as you find it.

See answers on page 219

In a Spin

As I spin on my wheel in Room 26, I can see Humphreyville, the incredible model town that my friends helped to build. Can you help too by matching up pairs of words that make the names of different places in Humphreyville? Draw matching lines from one side of my wheel to the other.

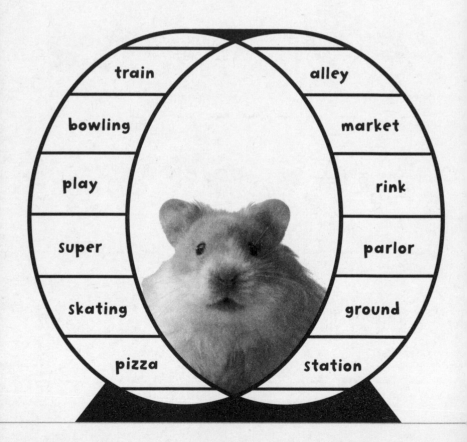

train

bowling

play

super

skating

pizza

alley

market

rink

parlor

ground

station

See answers on page 219

Finish the Job

When the class was building Humphreyville, our very own town, Mrs. Brisbane asked us to think about all the different and important jobs that people did in real towns. Here's the list of jobs we made. Can you guess what they are? Fill in the vowels—that's a, e, i, o and u—to complete the jobs.

1. T _ _ c h _ r

2. D _ c t _ r

3. N _ rs _

4. D _ n t _ s t

5. F _ r _ f _ g h t _ r

6. F _ r m _ r

7. B _ _ l d _ r

8. P _ l _ c _   _ f f _ c _ r

See answers on page 219

School Wordsnake

I've really gotten to know the students in Room 26 well during my time at Longfellow School. I can even spell all their names! Can you find their names in this winding wordsnake?

Use a pencil to draw a continuous line through the names in the grid (in the same order as the list below). The line will snake up and down, backward and forward, but *never* diagonally.

SAYEH   SETH

HEIDI   GARTH

ART   MANDY

GAIL   PAUL

RICHIE   A.J.

MIRANDA

S	A	Y	J	A
H	H	E	U	L
E	R	T	A	P
I	A	G	D	Y
D	I	A	N	A
R	L	I	H	M
I	I	E	T	R
C	H	M	G	A
A	R	I	H	T
N	D	A	S	E

See answer on page 219

Another Mysterious Message . . .

It was a very strange thing: one Friday morning, not a single person, not even Aldo, turned up at school. I couldn't work it out—then I looked out the window! I used Mrs. Brisbane's special letters to spell out the reason why. Cross out all the letters that appear twice, then rearrange the letters that are left over to find out why no one came to school that day.

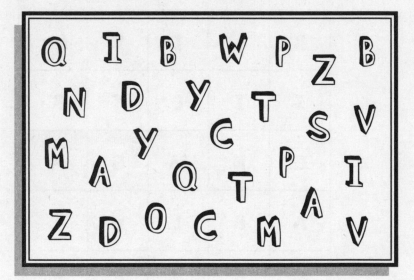

The reason why? _ _ _ _ _

See answers on page 220

Humphrey's Fabulous Food Jokes

I'm **LUCKY-LUCKY-LUCKY** that my friends in Room 26 give me my favorite treats, like yummy veggies and juicy fruits. These funny food jokes are making me hungry!

Q. Why were the strawberries upset?
A. They were in a jam.

Q. Why did the orange stop rolling?
A. It was out of juice.

Q. Why did the banana go to the hospital?
A. It wasn't peeling very well.

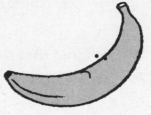

ha-ha!

Q. Why did the raisin go out with the fig?
A. Because it couldn't get a date.

**Q. What kind of fruit
has a short temper?**
A. A crabby apple.

Q. Which fruit likes riding roller coasters?
A. The ki-whee!

Q. What can bananas do that other fruit can't?
A. Splits.

Q. What fruit never gets lonely?
A. A pear.

PEAR/PAIR—do you get it? If you're a good speller, like me, it can really help with jokes!

Q. What do you give a hurt lemon?
A. Lemonade.

**Q. What did the banana
say to the elephant?**
A. Nothing. Bananas can't talk.

**Q. What do you get if you
cross an apple and a
Christmas tree?**
A. A pine-apple.

Q. How do oranges play baseball?
A. With fruit bats.

**Q. What's green on the outside but yellow
on the inside?**
A. A banana disguised as a cucumber.

Q. Why is a tomato round and red?
A. Because if it was long and green, it would be a cucumber.

Q. What type of jokes do vegetables like best?
A. Corny ones.

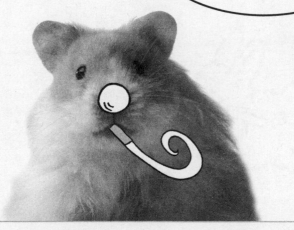

Like this one—what did the baby corn say to the mommy corn? Where's Pop corn?

Q. What did one tomato say to the other?
A. "You go on, I'll ketchup."

Q. What do you get if two peas start a fight?
A. Black-eyed peas.

Q. What's small, green and goes camping a lot?
A. A boy sprout.

Q. How do you know carrots are good for your eyesight?
A. Well, have you ever seen a rabbit wearing glasses?

Q. What do you call an angry pea?

A. Grump-pea.

I think I know what my classmates' favorite beans are—jellybeans!

Q. Why should you never tell a secret in a cornfield?

A. Because there are too many ears around!

Q. Which vegetable is green and strong?

A. A muscle sprout.

mmm!

Humans eat unsqueakably delicious foods! Once, Aldo slipped me a bite of pizza. I stored it in my cheeks for a midnight snack. YUM!

Q. What's the best thing to put on a pizza?
A. Your teeth.

Q. What do you call cheese that isn't yours?
A. Na-cho cheese!!

Q. Which cheese is made backward?
A. Edam.

Q. Why did the cookie go to the hospital?
A. It felt crumby.

Q. Where do hamburgers go to dance?
A. The meatball.

Q. What's the best way to eat turkey?
A. Gobble it.

Q. How do you make a hot dog stand?
A. Steal its chair.

Q. Where were potatoes first fried?
A. In Greece.

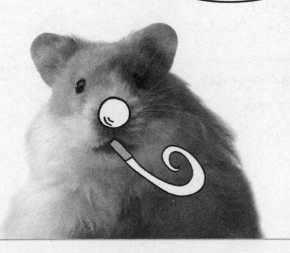

Did you hear about the OLD-OLD-OLD potatoes? They were fried in ANCIENT GREECE!

hee hee!

Q. What do you call a burger that runs away?

A. Fast food.

Q. What kind of snack swings from tree to tree?

A. A chocolate chimp cookie.

Q. What's the difference between boogers and broccoli?
A. Kids won't eat broccoli.

Q. What's white, fluffy and beats its chest in a cake shop?
A. A meringue-utang.

Q. What's the biggest dessert in the world?
A. The Trifle Tower.

> I've heard the best way to see the Trifle Tower is from the air—in a JELLYCOPTER . . .

Things That Make Humphrey Go "Eek"

My first Halloween was an eye-opening experience. I thought it would be scary, but, apart from some unsqueakably spooky pumpkins, it was really FUN-FUN-FUN! And so are these jokes!

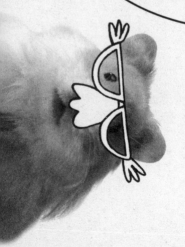

Q. What do hamsters do for Halloween?

A. Trick or Squeak.

Q. Why did the boy carry a clock and a bird on Halloween?
A. For "Tick or Tweet."

Q. What do fish do for Halloween?
A. Trick or Trout.

Q. What are baby witches called?
A. Halloweenies.

Q. What do werewolves celebrate in October?
A. Howloween.

Q. What do you call a pumpkin that's been dropped?
A. A squash.

As a small creature,
I'm scared of a LOT of things,
like witches and monsters
and—eeek! I think I'll just
go and hide in my sleeping
house while you read
these spooky jokes. . . .

Q. What would happen if you saw twin witches?

A. You wouldn't know which witch was which.

Q. What do you call witches who share a room?

A. Broom mates.

Q. What do you call a witch with one leg?
A. Eileen.

**Q. What do you call a witch
who throws up on bumpy journeys?**
A. Broom-sick.

Q. What has six legs and flies?
A. A witch giving her cat a lift.

**Q. Why did the witch give
up fortune telling?**
A. She couldn't see any
future in it.

Q. What do you get if you cross a witch with an ice cube?
A. A cold spell.

Q. How do you make a witch itch?
A. Take away the "w"!

I think "s" is the scariest letter—after all, it makes cream SCREAM!

WITCH 1: I bought one of those brand-new paper cauldrons.
WITCH 2: Any good?
WITCH 1: No, it was tearable!

Q. What's the first thing a witch does in the morning?
A. She wakes up.

Q. What do you call a nervous witch?
A. A twitch.

Q. What's evil, has a pointy hat and goes round and round?
A. A witch in a revolving door.

Q. What do you give a witch at tea time?

A. A cup and sorcerer.

Q. How do witches tell the time?

A. With a witch watch.

Q. How do witches keep their hair in place?

A. With scare spray.

All my friends dressed up in amazing costumes for Halloween so I decided to crawl under a cloth to be a hamster "ghost"! My friends thought I was funny and I even won a prize. It was BOO-TIFUL! Here are some more funny ghosts. . . .

Q. What do ghosts call their moms and dads?
A. Transparents.

Q. Why did the ghost go to the barber shop?
A. He needed a scarecut.

Q. What do ghosts have in their cars?
A. Sheetbelts.

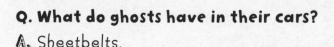

Q. What's the ghost's favorite theme park ride?
A. The roller ghoster.

Q. Why are graveyards noisy places?
A. Because of all the coffin!

Q. Where do ghosts go on holiday?
A. The Dead Sea.

Q. What happened when the boy ghost met the girl ghost?

A. It was love at first fright.

Q. What did the mommy ghost say to the baby ghost?

A. "Only spook when you're spooken to."

Q. Which is the ghost's favorite day of the week?

A. Moanday.

Don't forget FRIGHTDAY!

**Q. What do you get if you cross a ghost
with a bag of potato chips?**
A. A snack that goes "Crunch!" in the night.

Q. Who did the ghost get married to?
A. His ghoul friend.

**Q. What do you call a
prehistoric ghost?**
A. A terror-dactyl.

They say MONSTERS don't really exist, but that doesn't stop me shaking in my fur at the thought of one! Hope these jokes make you shake too— with laughter!

Q. What do you say to an angry monster?
A. "No need to bite my head off!"

Q. What's a monster's favorite soup?
A. Scream of tomato.

Q. Where do you find monster snails?
A. At the end of monsters' fingers.

Q. What do you say to a three-headed monster?
A. "Hello, hello, hello."

Q. What do you need if you go bungee jumping with a monster?
A. Really strong elastic.

Q. How do you know if there's a monster in bed with you?
A. By the big "M" on its pajamas.

What scares me even more than big hairy dogs? Big hairy drooling werewolves! Luckily, they only appear when there's a full moon—but you can laugh at these wolfish jokes whenever you like!

Q. What's scary, hairy and wears a pair of boxer shorts?
A. An under-wear wolf.

Q. What do you get if you cross a werewolf with a dozen eggs?
A. A very hairy omelette.

Q. What do you call the relatives of the werewolf?
A. The whenwolf and the whatwolf.

Q. Why are werewolves good at quizzes?

A. Because they always have a snappy answer.

**Q. What happens if you cross
a werewolf with a sheep?**

A. You'd better get a new sheep.

**I used to be a werewolf but I'm all right
nooooooooooooowwwww!**

HELP! Here are even more fur-raising creepies that make me want to hide away in my sleeping house!

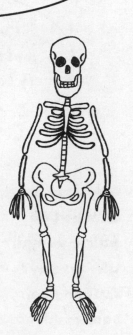

Q. Why are skeletons so calm?
A. Because nothing gets under their skin.

Q. What did one skeleton say to the other?
A. "If we had any guts we'd get out of here."

Q. Why didn't the skeleton go to the party?
A. Because he had no body to go with.

Q. What's a vampire's favorite fruit?
A. Neck-tarines.

Q. How does a vampire get into his house?
A. Through the bat flap.

I've heard that most vampires are very BAT-tempered....

Q. What do polite vampires always say?
A. "Fang you very much."

Q. What do you call a vampire who doesn't like the sight of blood?
A. A failure.

Q. What do you call a duck with fangs?
A. Count Quackula.

Q. What do vampires suck when they've got a sore throat?
A. Coffin drops.

Q. What did the vampire say when he saw a giraffe for the first time?

A. "I'd like to get to gnaw you."

Q. Why do vampires always use red pencils?

A. Because they're good at drawing blood.

Q. What comes out at night and goes "bite bite ouch"?

A. A vampire with a toothache.

Help Humphrey

I **LOVE-LOVE-LOVE** mazes, don't you? Garth and A.J. have built me a terrific maze, filled with confusing twists and turns. But it's a little too tricky—even for an especially clever hamster like me! Can you help me find my way out?

WAY OUT

See answer on page 218

Humphrey's Halloween Match-Up

I thought Halloween (or is it Howloween?) would be
scary at first, but then I realized it was **FUN-FUN-FUN**!
Playing Trick-or-Squeak, dressing up in costumes . . .
We even put on a great show!

Afterward, all the Halloween things were left in Room 26. There are two of everything. Can you match up the pairs by drawing lines? When you've finished, you will find one thing left over that has nothing to do with Halloween. What is it?

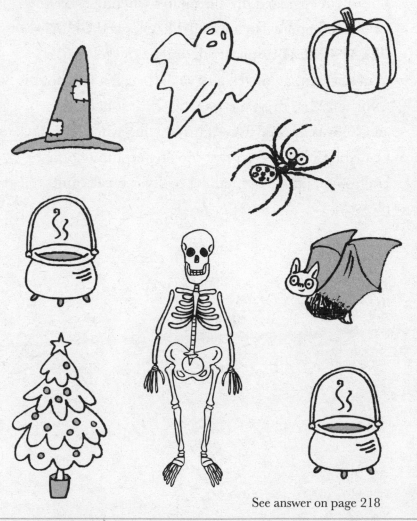

See answer on page 218

Humphrey's Halloween Costume

I hardly recognized my classmates when they were all dressed up for Halloween! They looked **GREAT-GREAT-GREAT** as pirates, a dragon, a skeleton, a mad scientist, an angel, a devil and even a cat (not my favorite). Mrs. Brisbane was the scariest of them all: she was dressed as a weird-looking witch! Spooky! Can you design me a great-looking costume for a Halloween party? Something really eye-catching, please!

Pumpkin Pairs

Halloween is a whole lot of fun, especially when everyone dresses up in costumes and goes trick-or-treating. But I try not to look at the pumpkin lanterns—I find them a little scary! Can you match up these five pairs of pumpkins by drawing lines between them? I can't do it—I'm covering my eyes with my paws!

My Dot-to-Dot Pal

Join the dots to find a friend that I can always count on.

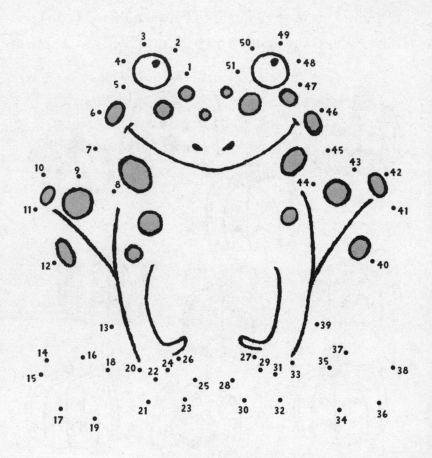

Humphrey's Favorite Frog Jokes*

As you know, **Og** the frog and I are good pals. We don't have much in common but he's always been a "toad-ally" loyal friend to me. So here are my special jokes for **Og**. I'm paws-itive they'll make him go "BOING"!

Q. What's Og's favorite flower?
A. A croakus.

Q. What's Og's favorite candy?
A. Lollihops.

*(dedicated to a favorite froggy friend)

Q. Where do frogs keep their money?

A. In a river bank.

Q. What animal has more lives than a cat?

A. A frog, because he croaks every night.

Q. What's green, slimy and found at the North Pole?

A. A lost frog.

What happens when a frog's car breaks down?
A. He gets toad away.

Q. How do frogs cheer?
A. Hop-hop-hooray!

Q. What do you say if you meet a toad?
A. "Wart's new?"

boing!

Or in Og's case, you could just say "BOING!" That's more his style.

Q. What goes "dot-dot-croak, dot-dash-croak"?
A. Morse toad.

Q. Where do frogs keep their treasure?
A. In a croak of gold at the end of the rainbow.

Q. What's white on the outside, green on the inside and comes with relish and onions?
A. A hot frog.

**Q. What kind of tiles can't
you stick on walls?**
A. Reptiles.

**Q. What would you say to a frog
who needs a lift?**
A. "Hop in!"

**Q. Where do frogs leave their
hats and coats?**
A. In the croakroom.

If Og wore a
hat and coat, he'd
make a big splash—
especially when he
went for
a SWIM!

Q. What kind of frog has horns?
A. A bullfrog.

**Q. What's green and can jump
a mile a minute?**
A. A frog with hiccups.

That reminds
me of the time I got
trapped under a bag of
snacks and Og jumped
ALL THE WAY out of his
tank to rescue me!
(And he didn't even
have hiccups).

ha-ha!

Q. What is a frog's favorite year?
A. Leap year.

Q. What's a frog's favorite music?
A. Hip-hop.

Q. Why was the frog down in the mouth?
A. He was unhoppy.

Q. What did the frog dress up as for Halloween?
A. A prince!

Much as I like Og, the things he eats drive me buggy! Unlike me, he prefers food that actually MOVES! So here are some bug jokes especially for Og. Eeew . . .

Q. What do frogs order in restaurants?
A. French flies.

Q. Why are frogs so happy?
A. They eat whatever bugs them.

Q. What happens when two frogs try to catch the same fly?
A. They get tongue-tied.

Q. What's a frog's favorite car?
A. A Beetle.

Q. Why was the cricket told to leave the park?
A. Because he was a litter bug.

Q. How do you know if a frog has ears?
A. Yell "Free Flies!" and see if he hops over!

eeew!

Q. What is a grasshopper?
A. A bug on a pogo stick.

**Q. What do you call a grasshopper
with no legs?**
A. A grasshover.

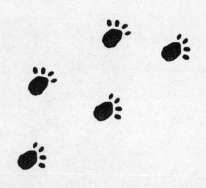

Q. What do you call two bugs that live on the moon?
A. Lunar ticks.

Q. Where do you put a sick insect?
A. In an antbulance.

I didn't know that—but I did know that you take sick wasps to the WASPITAL!

Q. What do you get if you cross some ants with some ticks?
A. All sorts of ant-ics!

Puzzling Pals

School's over for today, and I've just come out of my cage to visit my tank-dwelling pal, Og the Frog. Don't we make a handsome pair of classroom pets?

Look carefully at our two pictures, and see
if you can find six differences between them.

Humphrey's Odd One Out

Hmm . . . all these creatures in Pet-O-Rama may look the same, but if you look closely you'll spot a few differences. Can you circle one picture in each set of three that is the odd one out?

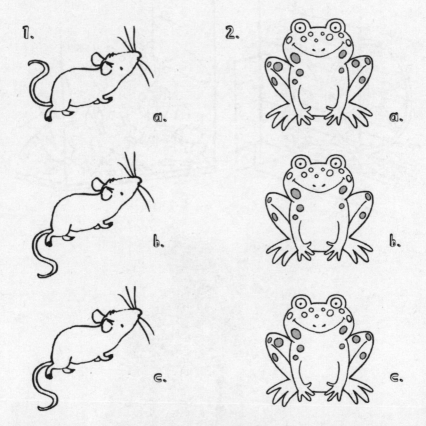

1.
a.
b.
c.

2.
a.
b.
c.

3.

a.

b.

c.

4.

a.

b.

c.

See answers on page 220

Og Dreams

My friend Og is a frog who doesn't say much, and sometimes I wonder what he's thinking about as he sits on a rock in his glass tank. What do you think Og daydreams about? Draw your idea in the thought bubble above Og's head.

Complete Og

I enjoyed Richie's birthday party, but I wasn't too impressed by Magic Mitch the magician. He had the nerve to make people's personal belongings completely disappear! Then (and this was very rude) he cut up Richie's dollar bill into lots of tiny pieces!

Now Magic Mitch has cut this picture of Og in half! Can you help by drawing the other half of the picture? *(Tip: it's a mirror image.)*

True or False Frog Facts

Before I met Og, my knowledge of frogs was nothing to squeak of. But since we've been sharing Room 26, I've been finding out a lot more about these amazing amphibians and how they live. How much do you know? Test yourself by reading the ten sentences below and ticking the true or false box. Just take a guess if you don't know the answer!

Boing!

1. Some frogs live in the ocean.
TRUE ☐ FALSE ☐

2. Frogs don't drink water—they absorb it through their skin.
TRUE ☐ FALSE ☐

3. A frog is a reptile.
TRUE ☐ FALSE ☐

4. Frogs eat insects such as flies, mosquitoes and crickets. TRUE ☐ FALSE ☐

5. A frog catches its food with its front legs.
TRUE ☐ FALSE ☐

6. Some frogs can jump up to twenty times their body length in one leap.
TRUE ☐ FALSE ☐

7. Frogs have terrible hearing.
TRUE ☐ FALSE ☐

8. A frog can change the color of its skin to blend in with its surroundings.
TRUE ☐ FALSE ☐

9. Only a male frog can croak.
TRUE ☐ FALSE ☐

10. A group of frogs is called an "army."
TRUE ☐ FALSE ☐

See answers on page 220

Ergh! What's Og's Snack?

It's safe to say that Og and I don't have the same taste when it comes to food. While I'm nibbling on my tasty fruit and vegetables, Og is more interested in munching . . . well, you'll have to do the puzzle to find out! Read the clues and write the names of all my favorite snacks in the grid opposite. Then you will find the name of Og's snack in the vertical box. **ERGH!**

1. An orange vegetable—rabbits love it too!

2. This is an occasional treat—much loved by mice and humans. You'll always find it on a pizza!

3. A delicious fruit that grows on trees and makes an excellent pie filling. Poor Snow White was poisoned by one.

4. Tasty little snacks that also grow on trees and come in many varieties, such as pistachio.

5. These small crunchy snacks are very healthy. If you put one in the ground and watered it, perhaps a plant would grow from it one day.

Yuck!

See answers on page 220

Humphrey's Painful Pet Puns

I remember my days at Pet-O-Rama, before dear Ms. Mac brought me to Room 26. Life wasn't too bad for me and my fellow pets. Our cages were clean and we had plenty of food and water. If only we'd had some of these great jokes to tell each other!

Q. What kind of pets just lie around the room?
A. Car-pets.

Q. What do you get if you cross a fly, a car and a dog?
A. A flying car-pet!

Q. Which pet makes the most noise?
A. A trum-pet.

I have a lot in common with fish—we both enjoy hanging out in SCHOOLS!

Q. Which day of the week do fish hate?
A. Fry-day.

Q. What do you use to catch fish in a library?
A. A bookworm.

Q. What do you call a fish that's eaten 24 carrots?
A. A goldfish.

Q. What fish can you see in the sky?
A. A starfish.

Q. What musical instrument could be used for fishing?
A. A cast-a-net.

Q. What's the best way to catch a fish?
A. Get someone to throw it at you.

Q. Why are fish so clever?
A. Because they live in schools.

Q. Why do fish avoid computers?
A. So they don't get caught in the Internet.

Q. Where do fish go for their holidays?
A. Finland.

hee hee!

I hear birds make good, inexpensive pets. Especially the ones going "CHEAP" at Pet-O-Rama!

Q. Why do hummingbirds hum?
A. They've never learned the words.

Q. How does a bird with a broken wing land safely?
A. With a sparrow-chute.

**Q. What do you get if you cross
a parrot and a centipede?**
A. A walkie-talkie.

Q. What do you give a sick bird?
A. Tweetment.

**Q. What do you get if you cross
a parrot and a lion?**
A. I don't know, but if it asks for a cracker,
you'd better give it one!

**Q. What do you get if you cross
a parrot and a cat?**
A. A carrot.

I always love a good joke—even if the joke's on me!

Q. Why did the hamster hide when it was raining?

A. Because it was raining cats and dogs!

Q. What's small, blue and furry?

A. A hamster holding its breath.

Q. What do you call a hamster with raisins stuffed in his ears?

A. Anything you like—he can't hear you.

Q. If you had five hamsters in one hand and seven hamsters in the other hand what would you have?

A. Massive hands!

Q. When do hamsters need oiling?

A. When they squeak.

Q. How do you get a sick hamster to the hospital?

A. In a hambulance.

Q. What should you do with a wet rabbit?

A. Give it a hare dryer.

Q. What do rabbits do after getting married?

A. Go on their bunnymoon.

I can't imagine having long ears like a rabbit. It would just be so . . . EAR-IE!

**Q. What do you call a rabbit
with no clothes on?**
A. A bare hare.

Q. What is a rabbit's favorite game?
A. Hopscotch.

Q. What do you comb a rabbit with?
A. A hare brush.

Q. What kinds of books do rabbits read?
A. Ones with hoppy endings.

Q. What's a twip?

A. What a wabbit calls a twain wide.

Q. What do you say to a rabbit who's going on vacation?

A. "Bun Voyage!"

Q. What do you call a very rich rabbit?

A. A millionhare.

Q. What do you call mobile homes for rabbits?

A. Wheelburrows.

Q. What do bunnies do when they buy a gift for someone?

A. Rabbit up nicely, of course.

Q. What did the magician say when he made the rabbit disappear?
A. "Hare today, gone tomorrow."

A magician once put me in his hat and tried to make me disappear. But I popped right out again! We hamsters like to "HAM" it up. . . .

Q. Who is the biggest mouse in the world?

A. E. Norm Ouse.

Q. What is small, furry and skillful with a sword?

A. A Mouseketeer.

Q. What kind of musical instruments do mice like to play?

A. Mouse-organs.

I like MICE.
They're small, like me,
so we always
see eye-to-eye!

Q. What's gray, furry and lives on a man's face?
A. A mouse-tache.

Q. What has six eyes but cannot see?
A. Three blind mice.

Q. What do you get if you cross a mouse with a can of oil?
A. A squeak that oils itself.

**Q. What do angry mice send
each other at Christmas?**
A. Cross mouse cards.

 Q. How do you get a mouse to smile?
A. Say, "Cheese."

When Golden Miranda
gives me a piece of cheese,
it makes me so happy I just
want to squeak "For CHEESE
a jolly good fellow"!

Q. When is it bad luck to be followed by a black cat?
A. When you're a mouse.

Q. What goes "dot, dot, dash, dash, squeak"?
A. Mouse code.

Q. Why do mice have long tails?
A. Because they'd look silly with long hair.

Describe Humphrey

I don't like to show off, but humans do sometimes say that I'm quite a handsome little fellow! Can you find and circle six other words that describe me? That will leave six words that really don't fit me at all!

FURRY   SLIMY   LARGE

CLEVER

FRIENDLY

SCALY

BORING

SMALL

CUTE

HELPFUL   HEAVY   UNKIND

Now finish the following sentence using the circled words:

I think Humphrey is _____

_____

See answers on page 216

Tasty Treats Wordsearch

Mmm, I have so many favorite foods that I love to snack on! My pal Aldo knows exactly what I like and always brings me a tasty little something. Yum! Can you find eight tasty hamster treats in this yummy, scrummy wordsearch? They might be up, down, across or diagonal.

APPLE • PEAR • CARROT • NUTS

SEEDS • CHEESE • RAISINS • BROCCOLI

S	E	L	P	P	A	C	P	B
T	R	A	U	A	H	U	N	R
E	O	S	E	E	D	S	T	A
E	C	B	E	F	C	E	P	I
A	P	S	L	B	A	C	K	S
S	E	G	I	R	R	E	U	I
T	A	U	H	A	R	I	E	N
B	R	O	C	C	O	L	I	S
C	E	M	A	S	T	U	N	W

See answers on page 216

Mixed-Up Pets

Pet-O-Rama is the shop where lovely Ms. Mac first found me. (Of course, my home is now in Longfellow School.) But all the pets I left behind have got their names mixed up—can you help to unscramble them?

1. t a c   _ _ _

2. o d g   _ _ _ _

3. e s u m o   _ _ _ _ _ _

4. r e b l i g   _ _ _ _ _ _ _

5. u n e g a i   g i p   _ _ _ _ _ _ _   _ _ _

6. s h e r m a t   _ _ _ _ _ _ _ _

See answers on page 217

Rodent Rampage

Uh-oh! All these rodent pets—hamsters, gerbils, mice and guinea pigs—have escaped from the pet store! Can you get them back to Pet-O-Rama before Carl the assistant discovers they're gone?

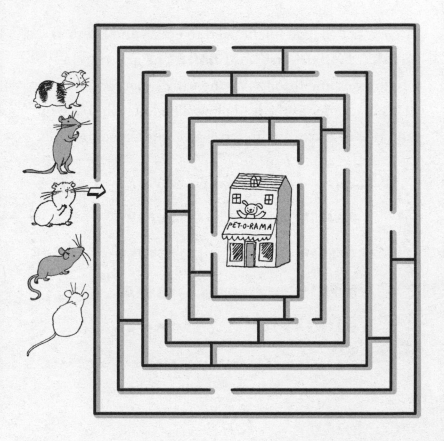

See answer on page 217

Pet Shop Wordsnake

Thank goodness there weren't any snakes at Pet-O-Rama, but here's a very different kind of snake—a wordsnake. (Believe me, this kind is much easier to deal with!)

Take a pencil (you might need to erase) and begin at **START**. Find the first word **HAMSTER** and trace a continuous line through all the words that follow, in the same order as the list below. The line will snake up and down, backward and forward, but *never* diagonally.

HAMSTER	PUPPY
GERBIL	KITTEN
MOUSE	PARROT
GUINEA PIG	RABBIT

START ⇨

H	G	E	T	I
A	R	R	B	B
M	E	L	I	B
S	T	M	R	A
S	U	O	T	O
E	G	U	R	R
P	A	I	A	P
I	E	N	E	N
G	P	P	T	T
P	U	Y	K	I

See answers on page 217

109

A House for Humphrey

I love my cozy cage, but sometimes it's fun to think about my dream house and what it might be like. At Pet-O-Rama, they sold some very fancy hamster homes—there was even a Chinese Pagoda and a **TALL-TALL-TALL** castle! Can you get creative and design a wonderful hamster house for me?

Name the Pet

I think the name "Humphrey" has a very nice ring to it, and it's the perfect name for a hamster since both words begin with "H"!

Can you give each of these pets a name that begins with the same letter as the animal, like "George gerbil"?

1. _____ cat

2. _____ dog

3. _____ rabbit

4. _____ mouse

5. _____ fish

6. _____ parrot

Humphrey's Hamster Challenge

Get your pencils ready—this challenge will get your brain spinning as fast as my wheel! How many words can you make using only the letters in the word below?

H A M S T E R

Write your words below. I've done one to start you off.

STAR

See answers on page 217

Mixed-Up Humphrey

Eek! All these words for parts of my body have gotten mixed up. Can you unscramble them and write the words in the spaces? Then draw a line matching the right word to the right part of my body.

eckeh

_ _ _ _ _

sone

_ _ _ _

yee

_ _ _

era

_ _ _

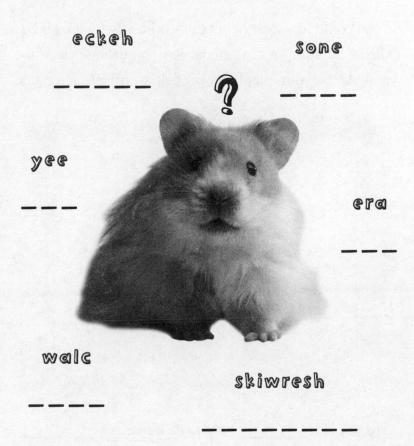

walc

_ _ _ _

skiwresh

_ _ _ _ _ _ _ _

See answers on page 219

My Favorite ♡ Pet

I **LOVE-LOVE-LOVE** being a pet! It's so great to be looked after and cared for by a human friend—and so interesting to find out about their lives, especially since they behave in very peculiar ways!

If you could have any pet in the world, what would it be? (Maybe a hamster? They make very rewarding pets, you know.) Draw your imaginary pet below and give it a name.

My pet is a _____   My pet's name is _____

Sleepy Wordsearch

Oh, I do love my naps! And my little sleeping area is so cozy and warm to snuggle up in after a hard night's spinning on my wheel! This very sleepy wordsearch contains eight sleep-related words. Can you find them? They might be up, down, across or diagonal.

SLEEP • BED • SNORE • YAWN
DOZE • NAP • PILLOW • DREAM

O	W	A	E	R	Y	A	D
P	I	L	L	O	W	B	N
A	S	Y	D	O	Z	E	R
N	O	B	R	P	A	I	S
E	W	Z	E	D	N	E	N
P	L	E	A	P	E	R	O
E	L	I	M	L	O	B	R
S	U	Y	A	W	N	A	E

See answers on page 218

True or False?

I've learned a lot about humans and their behavior by visiting the homes of my friends in Room 26. And they've learned a lot about me and how I live. In fact, I'd say they have all become hamster experts! How much do you think you know about hamsters? Find out by reading the ten sentences below and deciding if they are true or false.

1. **Hamsters are usually very good at escaping from their cages.**
   TRUE ☐   FALSE ☐

2. **Hamsters sometimes store food in their ears.**
   TRUE ☐   FALSE ☐

3. **When hamsters feel scared or threatened, they sometimes puff up their cheeks.**
   TRUE ☐   FALSE ☐

4. Hamsters are not very good at climbing.

TRUE ☐ FALSE ☐

5. Hamsters have long tails.

TRUE ☐ FALSE ☐

6. Other animals such as cats and dogs could harm a hamster.

TRUE ☐ FALSE ☐

7. The dwarf hamster is the smallest type of hamster.

TRUE ☐ FALSE ☐

8. In the wild, hamsters usually live in trees.

TRUE ☐ FALSE ☐

9. Hamsters are able to carry up to half their body weight in their cheek pouches.

TRUE ☐ FALSE ☐

10. Hamsters' teeth never stop growing.

TRUE ☐ FALSE ☐

See answers on page 218

Pet Picture Puzzler

Mmm, tricky! All these pet names fit into the grid opposite, but where do they go? Look at the pictures and write the words in the correct spaces. I've written in one (very important) letter to help you.

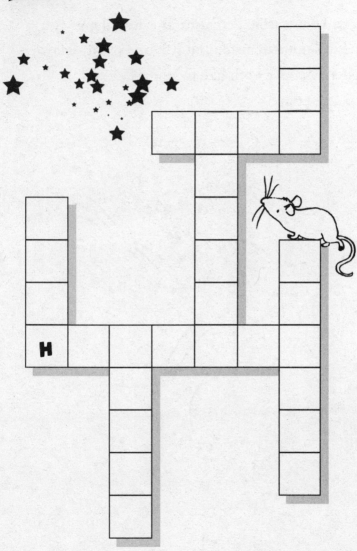

H

See answers on page 219

Dot-to-Dot Pet

Can you guess which creature this is? I'll give you a clue: it's not a hamster, but it is one of my fellow rodents—and we both like to squeak!

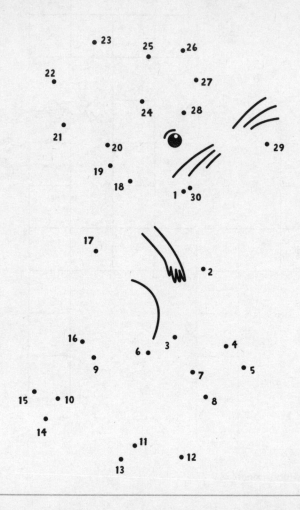

Trail of Treats

Oh, I'm hungry and I can't wait to get my teeth into a **YUMMY-YUMMY-YUMMY** snack! But only one trail leads to the apple. Can you choose the right one?

See answer on page 220

Humphrey's Haikus

I love living in Room 26 because Mrs. Brisbane is always teaching us new and interesting things. At the moment we're looking at haikus, an ancient form of Japanese poetry. Some of them are just like tricky riddles! Try reading these animal haikus (I wrote them in the little notebook I keep hidden in my cage) and see if you can guess which creature I'm describing.

So big and hairy
Long tail and a loud, loud woof!
Please keep off my cage!

ANSWER _____

Happy in his tank
Hops and jumps on long green legs
Can you hear a "Boing"?

ANSWER _____

Small, cute and furry
Watches humans from his cage
Spinning round his wheel.

ANSWER _____

Would you like to write your own animal haiku?
First, think of a creature you'd like to write about.
Then read these simple haiku rules and get creative!

HAIKU RULES

1. A haiku is very short—it has only three lines.

2. The first and last lines have five syllables, and the middle line has seven syllables. You can count them on your fingers!

3. Haikus don't have to rhyme.

MY ANIMAL HAIKU

_____

_____

_____

See answers on page 220

Humphrey's Crazy Cats and Daffy Dogs

Dogs are **NOT** my favorite creatures—especially Miranda's great big hairy beast, Clem. Believe me, his sharp teeth are no laughing matter . . . but these doggy jokes are!

Q. What's on special offer at Pet-O-Rama this week?

A. Buy a dog—get one flea!

Q. What happened when Clem went to a flea circus?
A. He stole the show.

Q. Why isn't Clem a good dancer?
A. Because he's got two left feet!

Q. What happens when it rains cats and dogs?
A. You might step into a poodle.

Q. What do you get if you take a really big dog out for a walk?
A. A Great Dane out.

Q. Why couldn't the Dalmatian hide?
A. Because he was already spotted!

ha-ha!

Q. Why did the dog cross the road?

A. To get to the barking lot.

Q. What do you do if a dog eats your pen?

A. Use a pencil instead.

Q. What do you get if you cross a dog and a cheetah?

A. A dog that chases cars—and catches them!

Q. Which dog loves to take bubble baths?

A. A shampoodle.

Q. What do you get if you cross a cocker spaniel, a poodle and a rooster?

A. Cockerpoodledoo.

And when it needs to poop, it's a Cockerpoodle**POO**!

Q. Why do dogs run in circles?

A. Because it's hard to run in squares.

Dog owner 1: I've lost my dog.
Dog owner 2: Why don't you put an ad
in the newspaper?
Dog owner 1: Don't be silly—he can't read.

Dog owner 1: Why is your dog going "meow"?
Dog owner 2: He's learning a new language.

**Dog owner 1: Why have you put
glasses on your dog?**
Dog owner 2: Because he's always barking
up the wrong tree!

**Q. What do you call a dog that thinks
he's a sheep?**
A. Baaaarking mad!

Q. What did the dog say when it sat on some sandpaper?
A. "Ruff!"

Q. What do you get if you cross a dog with a frog?
A. A dog that can lick you from the other side of the road.

Eeew, I HATE the thought of being licked by Clem. That mutt could really use some breath mints!

As you've probably guessed I'm not too crazy about cats either—anything bigger than me that likes chasing small furry rodents is not going to be my best friend! But I think you'll find these jokes A-MEW-SING!

Q. What kind of cat lives in an igloo?
A. An eskimew.

**Q. What do you get if you cross
a cat with a tree?**
A. A cat-a-logue.

**Q. What do cats like to eat
on a hot day?**
A. Mice cream.

**Patient: Doctor, doctor, I keep
thinking I'm a cat.**
Doctor: How long have you thought this?
Patient: Ever since I was a kitten.

**Q. Why couldn't the cat use
the computer?**
A. Because she ate the mouse.

Q. What kind of cat eats a lemon?
A. A sour puss.

**Q. What do you get if you cross
a cat and a canary?**
A. A cat with a very full tummy.

Q. How do you buy cat food?
A. Purr can.

**Q. What do you call a cat that has just
eaten a whole duck?**
A. A duck-filled fatty puss!

I'd rather not think about what cats like to eat— let's FURR-get I ever heard these jokes!

**Q. What do you call a cat who sails
the seven seas?**
A. Puss-in-Boats.

**Q. There were four cats in a boat, then one
jumped out. How many were left?**
A. None. They were all copy cats!

**Q. Which cat always knows
the right way to go?**
A. A compuss.

Q. How does a cat stop a DVD?
A. It presses "Paws."

I didn't know cats liked watching DVDs. I think they must enjoy MEW-sicals!

Q. What should you do with a blue cat?
A. Try and cheer it up.

Q. What kind of pasta do cats like?
A. Spa-catti!

**Q. What do you call a cat
with eight legs?**
A. An octopuss.

Q. What is a cat's favorite TV show?
A. The evening mews.

Q. What's a cat's favorite color?
A. Purr-ple.

purrr

There's another thing I don't like about cats and dogs—their **FLEAS!** Just thinking about them is making me itch!

Q. What is the difference between fleas and dogs?

A. Dogs can have fleas, but fleas can't have dogs.

Q. What did one flea say to the other flea?

A. "Shall we walk or take the dog?"

Q. Why are fleas the most faithful insect?
A. Once they find someone they like, they stick to him .

Q. How do you start an insect race?
A. One, two, flea—go!

Q. What did the clean dog say to the insect?
A. "Long time no flea!"

Q. How do you find where a flea has bitten you?
A. Start from scratch.

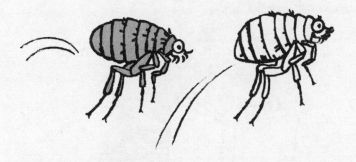

**Q. What do you get if you cross
a flea and a rabbit?**

A. Bugs Bunny.

Q. What did the romantic flea say?

A. "I love you aw-flea!"

Q. How do fleas travel?

A. Itch hiking.

Humphrey All at Sea

AHOY THERE! Not many hamsters can say that they've sailed on a tall ship. But when I nearly sank to the bottom of Potter's Pond I decided that a pirate's life was not for me. I still love hearing jokes about life on the seven seas though!

Q. What kind of ship doesn't sink?
A. A friendship.

Q. What kind of boat do you find in a garbage dump?
A. A junk.

Q. Three sailors fell out of a boat, but only two got their hair wet. Why?
A. The third sailor was bald.

Q. What do sea monsters eat?
A. Fish and ships.

**Q. Which are the strongest
creatures in the sea?**
A. Mussels.

Doctor, doctor, a crab just pinched my toe!
Which one?
I don't know—all crabs look the same to me.

Q. Which vegetable should you never take on a cruise?
A. A leek.

This is good advice for me, too—Mrs. Brisbane says it's BAD-BAD-BAD for hamsters to get wet!

Q. What did they call prehistoric sailing disasters?
A. Tyrannosaurus wrecks.

Q. What kind of stones are never found in the ocean?
A. Dry ones.

Q. Which bus crossed the Atlantic ocean?
A. Christopher Columbus.

Q. Why is it easy to weigh fish?
A. Because they have their own scales.

Q. Why do seagulls fly over the sea?
A. Because if they flew over the bay, they'd be bagels.

ha-ha!

Q. What do you find in a small ocean?
A. Micro-waves.

Q. How does the ocean say good-bye?
A. It just waves.

**Q. How do you communicate
with a fish?**
A. Drop him a line.

Q. What did Cinderella wear when she went swimming in the ocean?

A. Glass flippers.

Q. What is a mermaid?

A. A deep she-fish.

Q. What did the mermaid say when she was washed up on the beach?

A. Long time, no sea.

I think I know what mermaids would like for breakfast— MER-MALADE!

Q. What's the worst thing about being an octopus?

A. Washing your hands before dinner.

Q. Which fish can perform operations?

A. A sturgeon.

Q. What do you get from a bad-tempered shark?

A. As far away as possible.

Q. What lives in the sea and holds octopuses for ransom?

A. Squidnappers.

I think pirates are SCARY-SCARY-SCARY! But it must have been an exciting life, sailing the seven seas and shouting YO-HO-HO! I hope these jokes make pirates go HO-HO-HO instead!

Q. Why do pirates take so long to learn the alphabet?

A. Because they always get stuck at "C."

Q. Why couldn't the pirates play a game of cards?

A. Because they were sitting on the deck.

Q. What do you get if you cross a pirate's flag and a dessert?

A. A Jelly Roger.

Q. What was the lady pirate called?
A. Peggy.

Q. What do pirates like to listen to?
A. Opera—they like the high "C"s.

Q. Why do pirates carry a bar of soap?
A. So they can wash themselves ashore.

**Q. What do you call a pirate
who steals from the rich
and gives to the poor?**
A. Robin Hook.

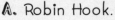

**Q. What do you get if you cross
a pirate with a pumpkin?**
A. A squashbuckler.

Q. Why is there a "d" in "bandana"?
A. Well, if there wasn't, pirates would be
wearing bananas on their heads.

I think they'd
look quite
A-PEELING!

Q. How much did the pirate pay for his earrings?
A. A buck-an-ear.

Q. How do pirates get to their ship?
A. By taxi crab.

Q. Why are pirates called pirates?
A. Because they aaaaaaarrrrrggghhhh!

yo-ho-ho!

The Wrong Hand Art Contest

My Wrong Hand drawing is a _____

On Wacky Wednesday Mrs. Brisbane had a fun
(and very wacky) idea. All the students had to draw
pictures with the hand they didn't usually draw with. It
ended up in a Wrong Hand Art Contest—and all the
drawings looked pretty strange! Why don't you have a
try? Draw something you are usually good at, but this
time with the wrong hand. How does it look?

Boat Bonanza

YO-HO-HO! I once took an unsqueakably dangerous voyage on a tall ship across Potter's Pond. It was a thrilling adventure! Here are six pictures of me in full sail. Can you spot one picture that is slightly different from all the rest?

c

d

e

f

See answer on page 221

Boat Wordsearch

My friends in Room 26 worked very hard to build their brilliant boats, and we all learned a lot about boats and ships at the same time. Here are eight different types of water vessel. Can you find them in the wordsearch below? They might be up, down, across or diagonal.

**BOAT • SHIP • FERRY • JUNK • YACHT
CANOE • LONGBOAT • SUBMARINE**

L	O	N	G	B	O	A	T	F	O
N	A	C	S	E	Y	G	P	E	T
E	J	U	N	K	A	J	N	R	A
R	C	B	Y	M	T	I	J	R	P
A	S	T	C	I	R	B	E	Y	T
K	N	A	H	A	H	O	R	Y	O
O	I	O	M	K	N	S	J	A	B
G	R	B	T	M	Y	O	G	C	I
Y	U	R	S	A	E	K	E	H	M
S	H	I	P	C	K	O	J	T	N

See answers on page 221

154

Design a Boat

Do you remember when the class built their own boats and sailed them across Potter's Pond? And I almost got a soaking—that was certainly a narrow squeak! The boats were all sensational: Miranda and Sayeh created a graceful swan, A. J. and Garth made a sailing boat with a skull and crossbones flag, while Art and Mandy built a Viking ship. Wow! Could you design a boat too—one that might win a prize for Most Beautiful or Most Seaworthy Boat? Draw your idea below.

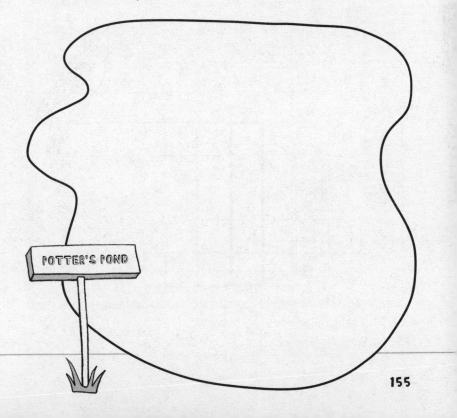

POTTER'S POND

Pirate Puzzle

Mrs. Brisbane has been telling us some fur-raising
stories about pirates! Now I know all about their
thrilling adventures sailing the high seas.

How much do you know about pirates? Try this
word puzzle and find out. If you get the five "across"
answers right, you will find a word that is something
you might have to walk if you were unlucky enough to
be captured by pirates. . . . Good luck, me hearties!

1. A bird that squawks and sometimes sits on a pirate's shoulder.

2. Pirates can't wait to get their hands on this! It's inside the treasure chest, along with glittering jewels and silver.

3. All pirates need one of these to guide them to the buried treasure.

4. A place where the treasure is usually buried. Pirates must sail here because it is completely surrounded by sea.

5. You will find this scary-looking symbol on a pirate flag.

Aaaarrr!

See answers on page 221

Oh, I can never get enough of hearing Mrs. Brisbane read us pirate stories! And I've learned lots of new words from them (like "Ahoy" and "Avast"!) Can you find eight words that pirates use in the wordsearch below? They might be up, down, across or diagonal.

SAIL • SKULL • RUM • TREASURE
ISLAND • PARROT • HOOK • SHIP

T	O	R	R	A	P	L	E	U
I	M	U	T	O	L	R	N	P
U	H	M	O	I	U	R	M	S
P	A	D	H	S	H	O	O	K
N	I	T	A	L	S	K	I	U
D	K	E	O	A	S	A	I	L
S	R	O	L	N	M	U	T	L
T	H	R	U	D	P	N	I	R
P	I	H	S	I	K	K	A	H

See answers on page 222

Pirate Dot-to-Dot

Avast matey! Join the dots to discover a pirate's favorite pet.

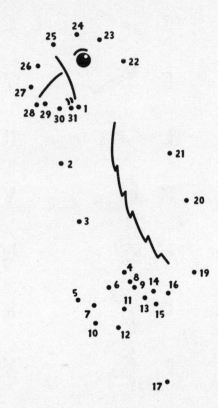

Humphrey's Pirate Secret Code

A    J   S

B   K   T

C   L   U

D   M   V

E   N   W

F   O   X

G   P   Y

H   Q   Z

I   R

Here's another of my **FUN-FUN-FUN** secret codes—
this time on a pirate theme. I got the idea from Mrs.
Brisbane's thrilling book, *Jolly Roger's Guide to Life*.
Can you work out what it is? I'll give you a clue: it's
something that pirates used to say. Write each letter in
the space as you find it.

_ _ _ _   _ _ _ _ _

_ _   _ _ _ _ _ _ _

See answers on page 222

Humphrey's Emergency Message

Once, when Aldo disappeared and a complete stranger took his place, I admit I got a little panicked. I decided to use Mrs. Brisbane's practice letters to spell out a message. Can you read it? Cross out all the letters that appear twice. Then jiggle around the remaining letters to spell out the message in the space below.

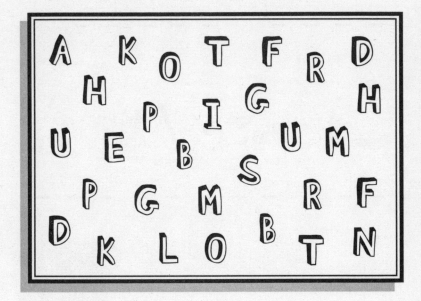

The message spells _ _ _ _ _ _ _ !

See answer on page 219

Humphrey's Nifty Knock-Knocks

I think all my classmates have names that are perfect for their personalities—just take a look at **PAY-ATTENTION-ART** and **SPEAK-UP-SAYEH** to see what I mean! Now here are some other names that are just perfect for a knock-knock joke.

Knock, knock.
Who's there?
Howie.
Howie who?
I'm fine—how are you?

Knock, knock.
Who's there?
Emma.
Emma who?
Emma bit cold out here, can you let me in?

Knock, knock.
Who's there?
Amanda.
Amanda who?
Amanda a spell, can you help me?

Knock, knock.
Who's there?
Howard.
Howard who?
Howard you like to let me in?

Knock, knock.
Who's there?
Noah.
Noah who?
Noah good place to eat around here?

Knock, knock.
Who's there?
Anna.
Anna who?
Anna gonna tell ya!

This is a great joke—if I told it to Stop-Giggling-Gail, I'm sure she wouldn't stop giggling all day!

Knock, knock.
Who's there?
Janet.
Janet who?
Janet has too many holes. The fish will escape!

Knock, knock.
Who's there?
William.
William who?
**William mind your
own business!**

Knock, knock.
Who's there?
Egbert.
Egbert who?
Egbert no bacon.

Knock, knock.
Who's there?
Wanda.
Wanda who?
**Wanda where
I've put my keys?**

This is
something
I hear humans
say A LOT!

Knock, knock.
Who's there?
Luke.
Luke who?
Luke through the keyhole—I'm here!

Knock, knock.
Who's there?
Howard.
Howard who?
Howard you like to hear a joke?

Knock, knock.
Who's there?
Sarah.
Sarah who?
Sarah 'nother way to get in?

Knock, knock.
Who's there?
Arthur.
Arthur who?
Arthur any more cookies?

Knock, knock.
Who's there?
Justin.
Justin who?
Justin time for dinner.

Knock, knock.
Who's there?
Amy.
Amy who?
Amy fraid I've forgotten.

Knock, knock.
Who's there?
Harry.
Harry who?
Harry up and get ready.

Knock, knock.
Who's there?
Toby.
Toby who?
Toby or not Toby, that is the question!

This is a famous line from a Shakespeare play called *Hamlet.* Or as I like to call it— "HAMSTERLET"!

Knock, knock.
Who's there?
Mikey.
Mikey who?
Mikey won't fit in the keyhole!

Knock, knock.
Who's there?
Sabina.
Sabina who?
Sabina long time since I've seen you!

I'd like to dedicate this knock-knock to MS. MAC. I wouldn't be a classroom pet without her!

Knock, knock.
Who's there?
Isabelle.
Isabelle who?
Isabelle working? I had to knock.

Knock, knock.
Who's there?
Sarah.
Sarah who?
Sarah phone I could use?

Knock, knock.
Who's there?
Omar.
Omar who?
**Omar goodness, I've knocked
on the wrong door.**

Knock, knock.
Who's there?
Stan.
Stan who?
Stan back I'm going to be sick!

Knock, knock.
Who's there?
Theodore.
Theodore who?
Theodore wasn't open so I knocked.

Knock, knock.
Who's there?
Shelby.
Shelby who?
**Shelby coming round
the mountain
when she comes....**

Knock, knock.
Who's there?
Ken.
Ken who?
Ken you let me in please?

Knock, knock.
Who's there?
Abby.
Abby who?
Abby birthday to you, abby birthday to you . . .

I just LOVE-LOVE-LOVE birthdays! Presents, cake, singing—it all makes me unsqueakably happy!

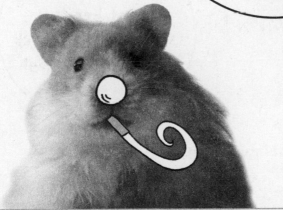

Knock, knock.
Who's there?
Alison.
Alison who?
Alison to the radio every morning.

Knock, knock.
Who's there?
Og.
Og who?
Og go to school every day!

And last but not least, here's a special knock-knock for a special frog!

Humphrey's Sleepytime Jokes

Like most hamsters I sometimes feel a little drowsy during the day. In fact, maybe I'll have a little nap while you read these very sleepy jokes. . . .

Q. Did you hear the joke about the bed?
A. It hasn't been made up yet.

Q. What do you call a sleeping dinosaur?
A. A dino-snore.

ZZZZZZZ

Q. What do you call a bull when it's asleep?
A. A bulldozer.

Q. What should you do if there's a monster in your bed?
A. Hide in the closet.

Q. Why did the boy sleep under the oil tank?
A. He wanted to wake up oily in the morning.

hee hee!

Q. Doctor, doctor, I can't sleep!
A. Lie on the edge of the bed and you'll soon drop off.

Q. Where do baby apes sleep?
A. Ape-ricots.

Being a hamster, I'd like to try sleeping in a HAM-mock!

Boy: Why are you taking a tape measure to bed with you?
Girl: I want to see how long I sleep.

Q. Where do fish sleep?
A. In a riverbed.

Q. Did King Arthur ever have bad dreams?
A. Yes, knightmares.

Q. What happens if you count sheep to help you get to sleep?
A. You have a baa-d night.

Q. How do you get a baby astronaut to sleep?
A. Rock-et.

Talking of "furry tales," why did Goldilocks fall asleep? She was at the house of the Three BORES!

Q. What kind of bedtime stories do pets like?
A. Furry tales.

Q. Doctor, doctor, I snore so loudly that I wake myself up!
A. Then sleep in another room.

Q. Doctor, doctor, every night I dream that there's a monster under my bed. What can I do?

A. Saw the legs off your bed.

Q. Why did Aldo run around the bed?

A. Because he wanted to catch up on his sleep.

Q. What does a cat sleep on?

A. A caterpillow.

Just PURR-FECT for a catnap!

Q. Where do big scary monsters sleep?
A. Wherever they want to!

Q. Why do you have to go to bed?
A. Because the bed won't come to you.

**Q. In which country do you get
the best night's sleep?**
A. Snore-way.

Humphrey's Color Wordsnake

Color is very important in my life. As you know, I am an unsqueakably handsome **golden** hamster. Og is a nice shade of **green**, while one of my favorite snacks, carrots, is a lovely bright **orange**. Can you trace all these colors in the grid opposite? Use a pencil to draw a continuous line through the words, which are in the same order as the list below. The line will snake up and down, backward and forward, but *never* diagonally.

GOLDEN	**BLACK**
GREEN	**BROWN**
ORANGE	**SILVER**
RED	**YELLOW**
BLUE	**PINK**

G	O	L	D	E
O	N	R	G	N
R	E	E	K	N
A	E	D	P	I
N	R	B	W	O
G	E	L	L	L
B	E	U	E	Y
L	R	O	E	R
A	B	W	V	L
C	K	N	S	I

See answer on page 220

Humphrey's Alien Antics

I found out **A LOT** about aliens when I watched a movie at Seth's house. Apparently, alien creatures talk a strange language and are green! That's just **WEIRD-WEIRD-WEIRD!**

Q. What are aliens' favorite sweets?
A. Mars-mallows.

Q. Why don't aliens celebrate Christmas?
A. Because they don't like to give away their presence.

Q. What's an alien's favorite drink?
A. Gravi-tea.

Q. What do space cows say?
A. "Mooooo-n."

Q. What is an alien's favorite board game?
A. Moon-opoly.

Q. What do you call a pan floating through space?
A. An unidentified frying object.

hee hee!

Q. What did the alien say to the garden?
A. "Take me to your weeder."

Q. What do aliens say when they meet each other for the first time?
A. "Pleased to meteor!"

But if an alien met me, he might say, "Pleased to eat you"! EEK!

Q. What songs do aliens like to sing?
A. Nep-tunes.

Q. What's the best way to talk to an alien?
A. From a very long distance.

Q. Where do aliens keep their sandwiches?
A. In their launch boxes.

Q. Did you hear about the alien who had eight arms?
A. He said they came in handy.

**Q. What sort of lights
do aliens have at
their homes?**
A. Satellites.

Q. What do alien children do at Halloween?
A. They go from door to door dressed up as
humans.

**Q. What do aliens put
on their cakes?**
A. Mars-ipan.

Q. What do aliens spread on their toast in the mornings?
A. Mars-malade.

Q. Where do aliens go to watch movies?
A. Cine-mars.

I like seeing films. Apparently cows do too—they're always going to the MOOO-VIES!

Q. What should you do with a green alien?
A. Put it in a bowl and wait until it's ripe!

Q. Where do aliens live?
A. In green houses.

Q. Why did the spaceship land outside the girl's bedroom?
A. She left the landing light on.

ALIENS look and act pretty strange and scary. But take it from a hamster—some humans do, too!

Q. Why are aliens so forgetful?
A. Because everything they hear goes in one ear and out of the others.

Q. Why did the alien get such good marks on his test?
A. Because two heads are better than one.

Q. What happened when the alien lost one of his arms?
A. He went to the second-hand shop.

Humphrey's Mad Mix-Up

It's time to put in all the jokes that wouldn't fit into any of my other sections. I call it my MAD MIX-UP!

Q. Why wouldn't the teddy bear eat any dinner?
A. He was stuffed.

Q. What did the hat say to the scarf?
A. You hang around while I go on ahead.

ha-ha!

Q. What do you get if you cross a toadstool with a suitcase?
A. Not mushroom for your clothes.

Q. What is smarter than a talking cat?
A. A spelling bee.

Q. Why did the boy ask his father to sit on the fridge?
A. He wanted an ice cold pop.

Q. What did one elevator say to the other elevator?
A. "I think I'm coming down with something."

Q. Why did the street light turn red?
A. Wouldn't you if you were caught changing in the middle of the street?

Q. What did one eye say to the other?
A. "Between me and you, something smells."

I know a great nose joke. What did the nose shout at the audition? **PICK ME!**

Q. Are those curtains real?
A. No—they're drawn.

Q. What do you call a truck that runs over your toe?
A. A toe-truck.

Q. What do you get if you cross a vampire with a mummy?
A. Something you don't want to unwrap.

Q. What do monkeys do at the theater?
A. They ape-plaud.

Q. What do penguins wear on their heads?
A. Ice caps.

Q. What do you call a penguin in the desert?
A. Lost!

That reminds me—what do you call a hamster in a bath? SQUEAKY CLEAN!

**Q. What do you call a pig
stuck in a pine tree?**
A. A porky-pine.

**Q. What do porcupines say
after they kiss?**
A. "Ouch!"

**Q. What did the pig wear to
the fancy party?**
A. A pig's-tie!

**Q. What do you call a bull you
can put in the washing machine?**
A. Washable.

Q. What do you call a train with a bad cold?

A. An achoo-choo train.

Q. What happened to the wooden car with wooden wheels and a wooden steering wheel?

A. It wooden go.

Q. What do you call a very old ant?
A. An ant-ique.

Q. What is the biggest ant in the world?
A. An eleph-ant.

Q. What's even bigger than that?
A. A gi-ant!

What do you call an ant with frog's legs?
AN ANT-PHIBIAN!

Q. Why was the centipede dropped from the football team?
A. He took too long to put his cleats on!

Q. What do you call a bee who is always complaining about something?
A. A grumble bee.

Q. How do snails get ready for a party?
A. They apply snail polish.

I once heard someone say that a slug was a HOMELESS SNAIL!

Q. What's the difference between a coyote and a flea?
A. One howls on the prairie and the other prowls on the hairy.

If I was ever unlucky enough to get a FLEA, I hope it would soon "FLEE"!

Q. Where do sheep get their hair cut?
A. At the baa-baas.

Q. What did King Kong say when his sister had a baby?
A. "Well, I'll be a monkey's uncle!"

Q. Why can't a bicycle stand up on its own?

A. Because it's two-tired.

Q. What do you call a broken boomerang?

A. A stick.

Q. Why did the house go to the doctor's?

A. It had a window pane.

Q. Who stole the soap from the bathroom?

A. The robber duck.

Q. What do you get if you cross an elephant and a fish?
A. Swimming trunks.

Q. Where do otters come from?
A. Otter space.

That joke is OTTER nonsense!

Q. What do you get if you cross a long-distance runner with an apple pie?
A. Puff pastry.

Q. What did the hungry computer eat?
A. Chips, one byte at a time.

Q. What did the mommy volcano say to the baby volcano?
A. "I lava you."

I expect mommy sheep say, "I love EWE"!

Do ducks wake up at the QUACK of dawn?

Q. What do you get when you put three ducks in a box?
A. A box of quackers.

A duck went into a shop and bought some bread. The cashier asked him how he would like to pay. The duck replied, "Just put it on my bill."

Q. How do you get down from an elephant?
A. You don't—you get down from a duck!

Q. What's more dangerous than pulling a shark's tooth out?
A. Giving a porcupine a back rub.

Q. Why was the mommy centipede so upset?
A. Because all her kids needed new shoes.

Q. What do bees comb their hair with?
A. A honeycomb.

Help Humphrey Get Home

As you probably know, my cage has a lock-that-doesn't-lock, so I can come and go as I please without anyone knowing. But now that I'm out, I can't find my way back! Can you help me get to my cage? And how many Nutri-Nibbles will I pick up along the way?

See answer
on page 222

Humphrey's Favorite ♡ Things

There are so many things in life that are **GOOD-GOOD-GOOD**! Can you guess what some of my favorite things are? If you get the correct answers going across the word grid, you will find another special thing that belongs to me in the vertical box.

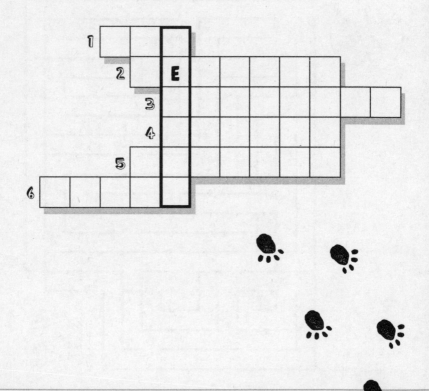

CLUES

1. I'm a nocturnal creature so there's nothing
I like more than to take a little _____ during
the day.

2. Mmm! I just love to nibble up these tasty, salty
snacks! Humans like them too—but sadly some have
an allergy to them.

3. I really enjoy writing in this. Then, afterward,
I hide it somewhere safe.

4. Oh yes! Another yummy
snack for me! This one is orange,
crunchy and very good for you.

mmm!

5. One of my favorite people in the class.
I call her "Golden," after her hair.

6. When I need exercise, I just take
a little spin in this.

See answers on page 216

Aldo's Word Ladder

I like watching Aldo as he does useful jobs around the school. But today he's got a tricky puzzle for you to solve! Read the first clue and change one letter in the word **RAT** to get the answer. Continue down the ladder in the same way but remember you can only change **ONE LETTER** each time. If you do it right, you'll end up with the same word that you started with.

1. Hamsters like it if you give them a gentle stroke or _____ .

2. Hamsters are a very popular _____ .

3. The opposite of dry is _____ .

4. You can catch fish with a _____ .

5. I like to eat a crunchy pea_____ .

6. A little house is sometimes called a _____ .

7. The opposite of cold is _____ .

8. Something you wear on your head is a _____ .

9. Change one letter and you'll get back to **RAT**.

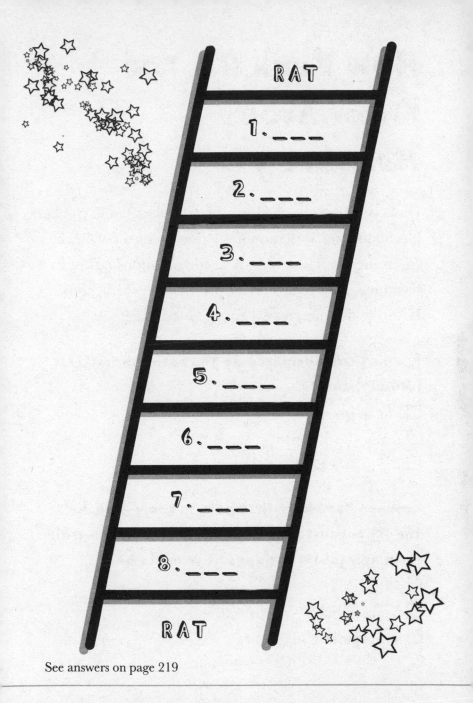

RAT

1. ___
2. ___
3. ___
4. ___
5. ___
6. ___
7. ___
8. ___

RAT

See answers on page 219

How Much Do You Know About Humphrey?

Have you read all the Humphrey books? Think you know lots about me? Well, now's the time to see how much you can remember! Take a look at the questions below. Each has three possible answers—just tick the correct box. If you're not sure, take a guess. Good luck!

1. What can Humphrey do that other hamsters (usually) can't?

☐ Fly a plane

☐ Read and write

☐ Play the piano

2. When Humphrey first gets to know Aldo, he's the school custodian. Then Aldo decides to train for a new job. What does he want to be?

☐ A teacher

☐ A scientist

☐ A magician

3. Who is the principal of Longfellow School?

☐ Ms. Mac
☐ Mrs. Brisbane
☐ Mr. Morales

4. What is Gail always doing in class?

☐ Grunting
☐ Giggling
☐ Gossiping

5. For Halloween, what did Humphrey dress up as?

☐ A ghost
☐ An alien
☐ A wizard

6. What pet does Golden Miranda own? (It's an animal that Humphrey really doesn't like.)

☐ A cat
☐ A snake
☐ A dog

How Much Do You Know About Humphrey? (continued . . .)

7. What is the number of the classroom that Humphrey lives in?

☐ 26
☐ 36
☐ 46

8. What kind of boat does Humphrey go sailing on during his Potter's Pond adventure?

☐ A pirate ship
☐ A Chinese junk
☐ A tall ship

9. Why does Miranda lose her job as the class animal keeper?

☐ She forgets to feed Humphrey.
☐ Humphrey gets out of his cage.
☐ She doesn't clean out his cage.

10. **What noise does Og the frog usually make?**

☐ Boing!
☐ Ribbit!
☐ Croak!

11. When Humphrey takes his first train ride, what does he almost crash into?

☐ A roller coaster
☐ A train station
☐ A lake

12. What fun and special day does Mrs. Brisbane think up for her class?

☐ Manic Monday
☐ Wacky Wednesday
☐ Fun-Fun-Fun Friday

Wow!
You really know a lot about me. I'm impressed!

See answers on page 222

Answers

p. 17 **What's in a Name?** 1. Speak-Up-Sayeh 2. Raise-Your-Hand-Heidi
3. Pay Attention-Art 4. Lower-Your-Voice A.J. 5. Stop-Giggling-Gail
6. Repeat-It-Please-Richie 7. Sit-Still-Seth 8. Wait-for-the-Bell-Garth

pp. 208–209 **Humphrey's Favorite Things**

```
1 N A P
    2 P E A N U T S
          3 N O T E B O O K
          4 C A R R O T
        5 M I R A N D A
6 W H E E L
```

p. 104 **Describe Humphrey.** The words that describe him are:
CUTE, FURRY, CLEVER, SMALL, FRIENDLY, HELPFUL

p. 105 **Tasty Treats Wordsearch**

```
S E L P P A C P B
T R A U A H U N R
E O S E E D S T A
E C B E F C E P I
A P S L B A C K S
S E G I R R E U I
T A U H A R I E N
B R O C C O L I S
C E M A S T U N W
```

216

p. 106 Mixed-Up Pets

1. Cat 2. Dog 3. Mouse
4. Gerbil 5. Guinea pig
6. Hamster

p. 107 Rodent Rampage

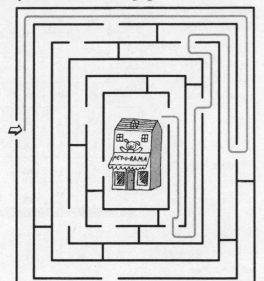

pp. 108–109 Pet Shop Wordsnake

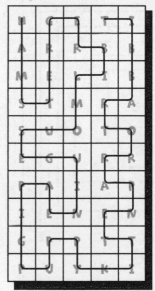

p. 112 Humphrey's Hamster Challenge

Here are all the words I found. Did you manage to find any others?

STREAM, EARTH, HEART, MARSH, MATH, SHAME, SMART, STARE, STEAM, EAST, HARE, HEAR, HEAT, MAST, MATE, MEAT, REST, SAME, SEAT, STAR, STEM, TAME, TEAM, TEAR, TERM, TRAM, ARE, ARM, ART, ATE, EAR, EAT, HAM, HAT, HEM, HER, MAT, MET, RAM, RAT, SAT, SEA, SET, SHE, TEA, THE

p. 18 Mrs Brisbane's Spelling Test

1. write 2. light 3. little 4. school 5. would
6. beak 7. different 8. because 9. believe
10. Wednesday

PP. 20-21
Humphrey's Rhyme Time

School, broom, boat, done, wet, dog. Miranda's pet dog is called Clem

PP. 116-117
True or False?

1. True
2. False—they store food in their cheeks.
3. True
4. False—hamsters are very good climbers.
5. False—hamsters have very short tails, sometimes you can't even see them!
6. True 7. True
8. False—in the wild, hamsters live in underground burrows.
9. True 10. True

PP. 62-63
Humphrey's Halloween Match-Up

The item left over is a Christmas tree.

p. 115 **Sleepy Wordsearch**

O	W	A	E	R	Y	A	D
P	I	L	L	O	W	B	N
A	S	Y	D	O	Z	E	R
N	O	B	R	P	A	I	S
E	W	Z	E	D	N	E	N
P	L	E	A	P	E	R	O
E	L	I	M	L	O	B	R
S	U	Y	A	W	N	A	E

p. 61 **Help Humphrey**

218

pp. 118–119 Pet Picture Puzzler

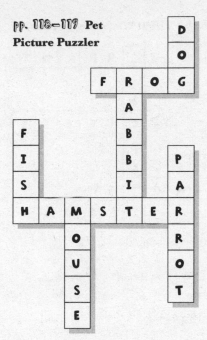

pp. 22–23 Humphrey's Secret Code

Message reads: **A FRIEND IS A PRESENT YOU GIVE YOURSELF**

p. 24 In a Spin

Train station, bowling alley, playground, supermarket, skating rink, pizza parlor.

p. 25 Finish the Job

1. Teacher 2. Doctor 3. Nurse
4. Dentist 5. Firefighter 6. Farmer
7. Builder 8. Police Officer

pp. 26–27 School Wordsnake

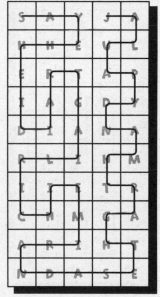

p. 113 Mixed-Up Humphrey

Clockwise: nose, ear, whiskers, claw, eye, cheek.

pp. 210–211 Aldo's Word Ladder

RAT, PAT, PET, WET, NET, NUT, HUT, HOT, HAT, RAT.

p. 162 Humphrey's Emergency Message Answer: ALIENS

pp. 80–81 Humphrey's Odd One Out

Answers: 1A, 2B, 3C, 4B.

pp. 84–85 True or False Frog Facts.

Answers: 1. False
2. True 3. False—frogs are amphibians
4. True 5. False—a frog catches food with its long sticky tongue.
6. True 7. False—frogs have very good hearing.
8. True 9. True 10. True!

pp. 86–87 Urgh! What's Og's Snack?

```
1 C A R R O T
  R
  I
2 C H E E S E
  K
3 A P P L E
4   N U T S
5   S E E D S
```

p. 121 Trail of Treats Answer: **B**

pp. 182–183 Humphrey's Color Wordsnake

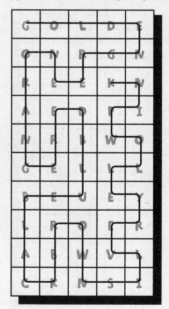

pp. 122–123 Humphrey's Haikus

1. Dog 2. Frog 3. Hamster

p. 28 Another Mysterious Message . . .

Answer: **SNOW**

PP. 152–153 **Boat Bonanza**

Answer: **D**

P. 154 **Boat Wordsearch**

L	O	N	G	B	O	A	T	F	O
N	A	C	S	E	Y	G	P	E	T
E	J	U	N	K	A	J	N	R	A
R	C	B	Y	M	T	I	J	R	P
A	S	T	C	I	R	B	E	Y	T
K	N	A	H	A	H	O	R	Y	O
O	I	O	M	K	N	S	J	A	B
G	R	B	T	M	Y	O	G	C	I
Y	U	R	S	A	E	K	E	H	M
S	H	I	P	C	K	O	J	T	N

PP. 156–157 **Pirate Puzzle**

	1	P	A	R	R	O	T
	2 G	O	L	D			
	3	M	A	P			
4 I	S	L	A	N	D		
	5	S	K	U	L	L	

221

p. 158 Pirate Wordsearch

T	O	R	R	A	P	L	E	U
I	M	U	T	O	L	R	N	P
U	H	M	O	I	U	R	M	S
P	A	D	H	S	H	O	O	K
N	I	T	A	L	S	K	I	U
D	K	E	O	A	S	A	I	L
S	R	O	L	N	M	U	T	L
T	H	R	U	D	P	N	I	R
P	I	H	S	I	K	K	A	H

pp. 160–161
Humphrey's Pirate Secret Code

Message reads:
AHOY THERE ME HEARTIES!

p. 207 Help Humphrey Get Home

Humphrey picks up five Nutri-Nibbles along the way.

pp. 212–215 How Much Do You Know About Humphrey?

Answers: 1. Read and write

2. A teacher

3. Mr. Morales

4. Giggling

5. A ghost

6. A dog

7. Room 26

8. A tall ship

9. Humphrey gets out of his cage

10. Boing!

11. A lake

12. Wacky Wednesday

Everyone's favorite classroom pet!

The World according to Humphrey

Betty G. Birney

Welcome to Room 26, Humphrey!

You can learn a lot about life by observing another species. That's what Humphrey was told when he was first brought to Room 26. And boy, is it true! In addition to his classroom escapades, each weekend this amazing hamster gets to sleep over with a different student. Soon Humphrey learns to read, write and even shoot rubber bands (only in self-defense). Humphrey's life would be perfect, if only the teacher weren't out to get him!

Everyone's favorite classroom pet!

Friendship according to Humphrey

Betty G. Birney

A New Friend?

Room 26 has a new class pet, Og the frog. Humphrey can't wait to be friends with Og, but Og doesn't seem interested. To make matters worse, the students are so fascinated by Og, they almost stop paying attention to Humphrey altogether! Humphrey knows that friendship can be tricky business, but if any hamster can become buddies with a frog, Humphrey can!

Humphrey to the Rescue!

Humphrey the hamster loves to solve problems for his class-mates in Room 26, but he never meant to create one! Golden-Miranda, one of his favorite students, gets blamed when Humphrey is caught outside of his cage while she's in charge. Since no one knows about his lock-that-doesn't-lock, he can't exactly squeak up to defend her. Can Humphrey clear Miranda's name without giving up his freedom forever?

Surprises for Humphrey!

A classroom hamster has to be ready for anything, but suddenly there are LOTS-LOTS-LOTS of big surprises in Humphrey's world. Some are exciting, such as a new hamster ball. But some are scary, such as a run-in with a cat and a new janitor who might be from another planet. Even with all that's going on, Humphrey finds time to help his classmates with their problems. But will Mrs. Brisbane's unsqueakable surprise be too much for Humphrey to handle?

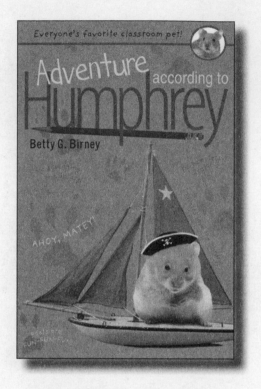

Humphrey Sets Sail!

Humphrey's friends in Room 26 are learning about the ocean and boats, and Humphrey can't contain his excitement. He dreams about being a pirate on the high seas; and when the students build miniature boats to sail on Potter's Pond, Humphrey thinks he might get his wish. But trouble with the boats puts Humphrey in a sea of danger. Will Humphrey squeak his way out of the biggest adventure of his life?

Everyone's favorite classroom pet!

The Haunted Howler

Camp is FUN-FUN!

The great outdoors

CAMP HAPPY HOLLOW

Owoooo!

SCRITCH SCRITCH SCRITCH

Summer according to Humphrey

Betty G. Birney

Humphrey Is a Happy Camper!

When Humphrey hears that school is ending, he can't believe his ears. What's a classroom hamster to do if there's no more school? It turns out that Mrs. Brisbane has planned something thrilling for Humphrey and Og the frog: they're going to camp with Ms. Mac and lots of the kids from Room 26! Camp is full of FUN-FUN-FUN new experiences, but it's also a little scary. Humphrey is always curious about new adventures, but could camp be too wild even for him?

Everyone's favorite classroom pet!

School Days according to **Humphrey**

Betty G. Birney

Roll-Roll-Rolling Rosie

Rules of School

It's the wrong room

Hurry-Up-Harry

Pop a wheelie!

Who Are These Kids?!

After an unsqueakably fun summer at camp, Humphrey can't wait to get back to Room 26 and see all of his classmates. But something fur-raising happens on the first day of school— some kids he's never seen before come into Mrs. Brisbane's room. And she doesn't even tell them they're in the wrong room! While Humphrey gets to know the new students, he wonders about his old friends. Where could they be? What could have happened to them?! It's a big mystery for a small hamster to solve. But as always, Humphrey will find a way!

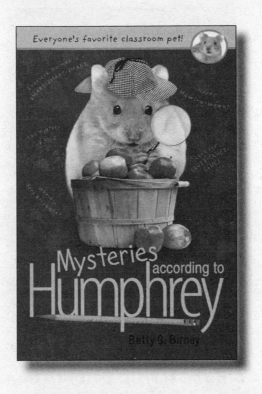

Everyone's favorite classroom pet!

Mysteries according to **Humphrey**

Betty G. Birney

EEK-EEK-EEK! Mrs. Brisbane Is Missing!

Humphrey has always investigated things, like why Speak-Up-Sayeh was so quiet and Tall-Paul and Small-Paul didn't get along, but this is a true mystery—Mrs. Brisbane is missing! She just didn't show up in Room 26 one morning and no one told Humphrey why. The class has a substitute teacher, called Mr. E., but he's no Mrs. Brisbane. Humphrey has just learned about Sherlock Holmes, so he vows to be just as SMART-SMART-SMART about collecting clues and following leads to solve the mystery of Mrs. Brisbane. . . .

A Hamsterific Celebration
of the Best Time of the Year!

Room 26 is abuzz. The students are making costumes and practicing their special songs for the Winter Wonderland program, and Humphrey is fascinated by all the ways his classmates celebrate the holidays (especially the yummy food). He also has problems to solve, like how to get Do-It-Now-Daniel to stop procrastinating, convince Helpful-Holly to stop stressing over presents, and come up with the perfect gift for Og the frog. Of course he manages to do all that while adding delightful heart and humor to the holiday season.

Room 26 Is Full of Secrets, and Humphrey Doesn't Like It One Bit!

So many secrets are flying around Room 26 that Humphrey can barely keep track. Mrs. Brisbane knows a student is leaving, but Humphrey can't figure out which one. (Even more confusing, Mrs. Brisbane seems unsqueakably *happy* about it.) The class is studying the Ancient Egyptians, and some of the kids have made up secret clubs and secret codes. Even Aldo is holding back news from Humphrey.

Humphrey's job as classroom pet is to help his humans solve their problems, but all these secrets are making it HARD-HARD-HARD!

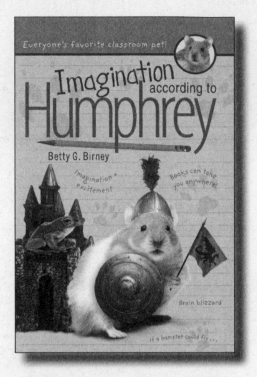

Even a Little Hamster
Can Have a Big Imagination!

Imaginations are running wild in Mrs. Brisbane's class, but Humphrey is stumped. His friends are writing about where they would go if they could fly, but Humphrey is HAPPY-HAPPY-HAPPY right where he is in Room 26. It's pawsitively easy for Humphrey to picture exciting adventures with dragons and knights in the story Mrs. Brisbane is reading aloud. If only his imagination wouldn't disappear when he tries to write. Luckily, Humphrey likes a challenge, and Mrs. Brisbane has lots of writing tips that do the trick.

Meet Humphrey!

Everyone's favorite classroom pet!

Want more FUN–FUN–FUN?

Find fun Humphrey activities and teachers' guides at www.penguin.com/humphrey.

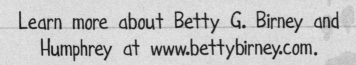

Learn more about Betty G. Birney and Humphrey at www.bettybirney.com.